Gardening

The Ultimate 2 in 1 Guide to Mastering Aquaponics and Permaculture!

2 Books in 1

Book # 1 – Aquaponics

Book # 2 – Permaculture

Copyright © 2015

All rights reserved. No part of this book may be reproduced in any form without permission in writing from the author. Reviewers may quote brief passages in reviews.

Disclaimer

No part of this publication may be reproduced or transmitted in any form or by any means, mechanical or electronic, including photocopying or recording, or by any information storage and retrieval system, or transmitted by email without permission in writing from the publisher.

While all attempts and efforts have been made to verify the information held within this publication, neither the author nor the publisher assumes any responsibility for errors, omissions, or opposing interpretations of the content herein.

This book is for entertainment purposes only. The views expressed are those of the author alone, and should not be taken as expert instruction or commands. The reader of this book is responsible for his or her own actions when it comes to reading the book.

Adherence to all applicable laws and regulations, including international, federal, state, and local governing professional licensing, business practices, advertising, and all other aspects of doing business in the US, Canada, or any other jurisdiction is the sole responsibility of the purchaser or reader.

Neither the author nor the publisher assumes any responsibility or liability whatsoever on the behalf of the purchaser or reader of these materials.

Any received slight of any individual or organization is purely unintentional.

Book # 1

Aquaponics

The Ultimate Guide to Growing Vegetables and Raising Fish with Aquaponic Gardening

Table of Contents

Introduction

Chapter 1: What is Aquaponics

Chapter 2: What Vegetables and Fish Do Well In Aquaponics

Chapter 3: Is an Aquaponic System Pest Free?

Chapter 4: Did You Know That Fish Can Suffer Stress And Die?

Chapter 5: A Simple Way to Start Off Your Aquaponic Farming

Conclusion

Introduction

I want to thank you and congratulate you for downloading the book, Aquaponics.

This book contains proven steps and strategies on how to rear fish and grow crops, particularly vegetables, within the same habitat. It identifies the plant and fish species that do best in aquaponic farming.

You will learn how to organically deal with pests and parasitic attacks, and also how to deal with varying pH levels and environmental temperatures. You will also see a list of nutrients that a plant normally requires in order to grow well. This book literally gives you all the information you need to start your own aquaponic farming.

Thanks again for downloading this book, I hope you enjoy it!

Chapter 1

What is Aquaponics?

Does this name sound very scientific, or is it just me? Incidentally, this hi-tech sounding name carries a very simple meaning: utilizing waste from water creatures to grow plants. So, waste from water animals – or more respectful, aquatic animals - becomes food for plants. Aquaponics is actually one of the ways to optimize the resources available to provide food with invaluable nutrients to people.

Of course, there is something unique about the whole process of growing the plants because you do not need earth, as in soil. In short, in this very unique process, the plants grow in water just like fish do; they call it hydroponics. This *hydroponics* also sounds very scientific but at least you know *hydro* is something to do with water; so it will not leave you bewildered.

So this farming technique uses liquid to produce vegetables and suchlike food, just the same way we use water to rear fish. And we are talking of plants that would ordinarily grow on land; the ones referred to as terrestrial plants.

Will any water suffice in aquaponics?

No and yes. Meaning? The water could be from a river, lake or dam, but the most important aspect is the composition of nutrients in that water. Normally you know clean water has just a few minerals that include mainly hydrogen and oxygen, as in H_2O, and those are, obviously, insufficient to grow your vegetables from tender seedlings to the dining table. So, clearly, the water used in aquaponics needs to be richer. And that is where animal refuse comes in.

How animal farming helps in plant farming

Aquaponic lies in between aquaculture and hydroponics. And remember we mentioned that aquaponics utilizes animal refuse as plant food. Now, if you notice, aquaponics and aquaculture have a similar beginning. The aqua part indicates that both deal with water or liquid material. Aquaculture nurtures both water living animals and water living plants in order to produce food; and its geographical zone is broad and varied - including wild habitat like ocean and sea coastal areas. Hydroponics, on its part, deals solely with nurturing of plants in a watery environment that could sometimes have sand or gravel; still for the purpose of producing food. Now the place of mutual benefit is what we are calling aquaponics.

Why marry aquaculture and hydroponics to get aquaponics?

As mentioned above, this is an issue of optimizing the available resources. It is important to keep the cost of production as low as possible if we are to feed the world adequately and in a healthy way.

For example, in hydroponics, it takes a big wallet to be able to supply the plants with all the necessary nutrients. In any case, you have got to buy them. Incidentally, these nutrients can go up to 20 in number, and the only ones that you do not need to buy are the ones that the natural water provides; namely, oxygen, hydrogen and carbon. Just think of the following nutrients that you need to enrich your water when doing hydroponics:

Macronutrients	Micronutrients (Essential Trace Elements)	Other useful minerals
Nitrogen	Chloride	Cobalt
Phosphorus	Copper	Silicon
Potassium	Boron	
Calcium	Iron	

Magnesium	Manganese	
Sulphur	Sodium	
	Zinc	
	Nickel	
	Molybdenum	

Then again, you cannot go on pumping sodium, phosphorous, copper, potassium, chloride, zinc, and all those other nutrients endlessly, and expect the environment to remain still healthy for the plants. Not with the whole process of food synthesis and release of by products by the plants. So, understandably, there is need to periodically flush the systems in order to dispose of waste. These processes not only call for consistent injection of money into the project, but also time.

Then there are the challenges on the part on aquaculture. This one now calls for daily attention: clearing some portions of water as a way of dealing with excess nutrients in the liquid. This is not cheap either, especially when it comes to labor and supply of water; hence, the logic in merging the two farming technologies.

So how, exactly, does aquaponics cost you less to farm?

Here it is. You have your fish in the usual place: tank, pond or such other place. As life continues, the fish are feeding and relieving themselves, because you obviously supply them with food. Do you know what would happen if that water remained intact for long? You would soon lose your fish due to toxicity. But in aquaponics, you have an outlet from your fish habitat, which carries the water with fish refuse to the plants' hydroponic tray. The plants flourish from the richness of that water, and as they consume the nutrients, the water becomes cleaner. That water is soon clean enough for the fish to dwell in; and, at that juncture, it is let back into the fish dwelling. So, in aquaponics, the fish benefit the plants and the plants benefit the fish – all to your advantage.

Chapter 2

What Vegetables and Fish Do Well In Aquaponics?

Ever had a waiter come to your table to ask what you preferred to have, without any concern that there was no menu within site? Funny, it appears; but it does happen. Here, we do not want to do the same, leaving you to imagine what you could grow even with no idea what is possible and what is not.

Here are some plants that do well in aquaponics:

A.   These plants grow easily and conveniently using aquaponics.

Type of Plant	**Type of Plant**
Leafy lettuce of any kind	Chives
Kale	Watercress
Swiss Chard	Mint
Basil	Pak Choi
Arugula	Many other house plants

B. Other plants that grow in aquaponics but demand an extra rich environment:

Type of Plant	Type of Plant
Tomatoes	Pepper
Cucumber	Beans
Peas	Squash
Broccoli	Cauliflower
Cabbage	

Considering how important vegetables and beans are in terms of nutrients required for good health, aquaponics is, definitely, a technique you would want to know.

And as usual, agricultural scientists are always experimenting, not only to upgrade plant and animal species, but also to see what different species will survive in different environments. In that regard, let us look at a group of plants that big firms like Nelson and Pade, Inc. have managed to grow using cost-effective method:

C.

Type of Plant	Type of Plant
Bananas	Onions
Sweet Corn	Beets
Micro Greens	Carrots
Radishes	Lemon
Lime	Oranges
Orchids	Violas
Nasturtium	Dwarf Pomegranate Tree

D.

In Aquaponics both the fish and the plants are equally important. Before we look at the specifics of the fish/plant relationship, let us look at the species of fish that have been tried in aquaponics and done exemplary well.

Fish Species	Fish Species
Tilapia	Pacu
Sunfish	Koi
Fancy Goldfish	Crappie
Blue Gill	Angelfish
Guppies	Tetras
Swordfish	Mollies
Many other ornamental fish	

E. Agriculture is an ever improving sector and, through aquaponics, other not-so-common fish have been bred and reared.

Below are some of them:

Fish Species	Fish Species
Barramundi	Carp
Yellow Perch	Catfish

Large Mouth Bass	Golden Perch
Silver Perch	

Chapter 3

Is an Aquaponic System Pest Free?

Surely no part of the world lacks irritants. Even the market with all its mirthful chatter has its mad man (or woman). So even the plants you are trying to grow will sometimes have a caterpillar here and there, or some of those parasitic elements like fungi. The good part of aquaponics is that you can solve most of these pest issues organically. So your fish remain safe from toxicity, and your consumers' health is protected too.

Here is how you can deal with pests in aquaponics:

A. <u>**Plants**</u>

   a Caterpillars

When you see these wiggling or crawling creatures trying to sample your plants like they were connoisseurs of sorts, all you need is this soil borne bacteria that is entirely natural, and you apply it. You can buy it in various outlets that specialize in aquaponic related products; often labeled *organic*. This category of bacteria is known as *Bacillus thuringiensis* and it is sold in form of a spray.

b   Insect which suck plant sap

These are particularly dangerous because sucking sap from your plants is like draining life out of them. So you need to ensure those pests are nowhere within your plant area. This, you do, by spraying natural pesticides like garlic based sprays. And do not for a moment think that chilli is only hot on your tongue; it is also used, in form of a spray, to burn off those pests. But note: moderation is it – do not overspray your plants. Like everything else, an overdose is never helpful.

c   Mould and fungi

These are parasites that can mess up your farming if you are not keen. But, of course, you cannot be an aquaponic farmer and not be serious. So you will, obviously, note the onset of a fungal attack and address it fast. All you need is a spray that is based on Potassium bicarbonate and your plants are safe.

All these sprays are available commercially; just check that you do not buy from quacks; buy from credible vendors and note the writings on the label to ensure you are dealing with organic stuff.

d   Slugs

How have heard of men (rarely women – I think) who have been drugged and robbed? Or let us say overfed with booze and then robbed and ditched someplace? A terrible thing to happen to anyone: but it is recommended you do that to slugs if they prove to be irritants in your farming endeavor. And how do you do that? That is fun: find a small saucer. Fill it in with beer – it does not have to be your favorite brand, of course. Some cheap stuff from down the street alley will do. Place the beer-filled saucer somewhere around the plants. These not-so-appealing creatures will crawl to the saucer; apparently the smell attracts them. After that, no other science is required: they just drown, and your problem is gone.

    e   Other irritants like aphids; thrips; and whiteflies

Strategically lay out some sticky straps that are colored. These pests will just stick on them as they move in targeting your plants.

Among the advantages of aquaponics is the room you have for DIY (Do It Yourself). It makes crop management relatively cheap.

B. Fish

Fish, too, are not without enemies; only, like plants, their enemies are manageable. If you ever have a problem with your fish, it will usually be due to one or more of these situations:

a) Ammonia Toxicity

How do you know the environment if toxic in this way?

As is expected, you are an observant farmer. So you will notice:

- Your fish seem lethargic
- They have visible red streaks on their body; sometimes on their fins
- They seem to be gasping for breath
- Their gills are red; in fact, inflamed.
- Their appetite is down

b) Fungal infection

You will easily see that your fish have this fungal attack by just looking at them. Here are the signs:

- White botches on the bodies of the fish
- White botches on their fins

c) Low level of oxygen in the water

This situation is a case of dissolved oxygen being lower than it is necessary for the survival of your fish. Here is how to know there is trouble:

- Fish begin to drop dead, one after another
- You see your fish struggling to breath
- As the weather turns hot, you realize your fish are dying even faster
- In the morning, you realize you have overnight fish fatalities
- You can see algae in your pond, fish tank or whatever fish rearing facility you are using

How do you deal with natural attacks on fish?

Well, the best and simplest way to avoid the problems of disease is rearing a species that is hardy; fish that is not prone to disease, and fish that is not prone to pests. This is because most diseases may call for curative measures that require chemical medicines, which is something you would like to avoid for a number of good reasons. These reasons include:

i) You can authoritatively tell buyers that your fish are strictly organically reared. And that, in addition to guaranteed market, is bound to raise your price a notch higher.

ii) You do not want to use chemicals that are likely to be in the fish even as you eat it.

But if you are really pressed, you can go for Potassium bicarbonate, which is a natural fungicide. It is eco-friendly and its label as you buy it should indicate that.

What are some of the hardy fish species?

You will be right to talk of these two fish species as hardy when it comes to disease:

- Jade Perch
- Silver Perch

Chapter 4

Did you know that fish can suffer stress and die?

First of all let us admit that it would be sad to lose fish when using aquaponics because that would be tantamount to losing the plants as well; of course, due to the inter-dependence. Secondly, it is costly to counter the effects of stress on fish, because, as in human beings, stress drags along other ailments, some which are fatal.

This is how you deal with situations that stress your fish:

Stressful Situation	How the stressful situation is	Solution
Shortage of oxygen in the water	This is the situation that gets your fish gasping for breath; and sometimes dying	• Aerate the water mechanically • Simply introduce an aerator
Excess solids in the water	In this situation, solids, mostly from	• Ensure more clean water is being

	excretion, accumulate and begin to raise the level of ammonia in the water. This high concentration of ammonia causes oxygen levels to fall. So the fish can get ill or just begin to drop dead.	pumped into the fish dwelling, possibly by having a branch from the main pump lead back to improve water circulation. In any case, with proper and continuous circulation of water, the solids are bound to float, making it easy to remove them.
Excessive nutrients	Usually, the culprit here is ammonia. The breaking down of the protein part of the fish feed serves to increase ammonia in the water. Also rising temperatures and	• Add lemon juice to lower the water pH. • Reduce the fish food rations, even as you speed up the entry of fresh water into the fish dwelling.

	rising pH levels increase the generation of ammonia. And once the ammonia level is too high, your fish are in danger of death.	• You could remove some fish thus reducing refuse and, hence, ammonia.
Origin of water	If you have water that is too chlorinated, like that one that is distributed in many cities, your fish will be in trouble.	• Dechlorinate the water before allowing it in the fish area. • Otherwise, stick to tank water, which is relatively safe.
Algae	Algae raise your water pH. In addition the science of how algae	• Get rid of algae from the water. • Get rid of sunlight

| | releases oxygen into the water is not fish friendly; a lot of oxygen in the day and none at night. | from your fish tank; this will make it unfavorable for algae. To do this, you can paint your tank. Also in building your tank, you can decide to use impervious material for the tank walls. |

Chapter 5

A Simple Way to Start Off Your Aquaponic Farming

Once you go beyond the scientific and botanical terminologies, which in any case are relatively few in this area, you will be able to embark on your aquaponic farming with minimal assistance. We need to begin by looking at the available options of aquaponic farming systems and their benefits.

Different Aquaponic Systems and Their Advantages

Farmers are not homogenous; fish are not; and even plants are not. So, it is a good idea to be able to choose how to rear your fish as an individual, and also how to go about manning your plants. For that reason, we shall analyze the major systems of aquaponics in use, and you can then take advantage of the one that suits your circumstances.

1. Media-filled beds

These are the simplest. For the plant zone, you just get a massive container and fill it with a medium of rock made of expanded clay or something that close. It is the place that you will allow water from the fish dwelling to flood and then you clear it; or even let the water flow continuously.

2. NFT, standing for Nutrient Film Technique

Though not very common, some farmers still opt to use this system. It involves small gutters that are enclosed within the crop farming area, and the nutrient rich water from the fish dwelling flows through in a thin film. Each individual plant stands in a tiny cup made of plastic, and only its roots dip into the water. This method is limited to a great extent in the variety of plants it can handle, and this is simply because of the expanse of the root system. Plants like the leafy greens and plants that are bigger in size may not do well in this system.

3. DWC, standing for Deep Water Culture

Here, you have a place where water from the fish dwelling is flowing into. Then you have plants within a floating raft – possibly a foam raft. The roots of the plants will literally be floating in water and pulling in the rich nutrients as the plants flourish.

Other times, the floating raft where the plants are is simply placed atop the fishing tank. The former technique is, however, more favored by farmers.

So, now, how do you go about establishing your system and proceeding to farm?

1) Identify the media bed that you want

For a beginner, DWC is convenient and relatively easy to use. This is because the media bed does all the important functions at once. This is how it goes:

- Removes mechanical solids by filtering the water
- Mineralization, which is basically breaking down solids and cycling of water
- Biofiltration

2) Decide how big you want your grow bed to be

Whatever size of grow bed you settle on, just have in the mind the standard depth of that area, which is 30cm deep. With such depth, it is unlikely that the roots of any plant will be inhibited by depth. So the plants will absorb enough nutrients to make them healthy.

3) Decide what size of fish tank you want

Even with all the liberty to choose, experts advise that you make 1,000 liters your minimum capacity for your tank. As a beginner, and possibly a layman, they say the bigger the tank, the more room you have to make mistakes and not harm your fish. They estimate that a single fish of 30cm in length is comfortable being within 200 liters of water.

4) Be careful about the ratio of your tank size to Grow area

Consider the volume of the two: Grow bed to fish tank, and begin with a ratio of 1:1. After all, you want to be cautious in everything, especially when you are new to this system of farming. Of course, you will learn more than a few things in the first few months, and in due course, possible within 4mths – 6mths, you will ready to raise the ratio to 2:1.

5) Mind the number of fish

Mark you aquaponics is not a license to imprison fish; they need to be able to swim freely – eating, playing (if they do), and living as near as possible to a natural habitat. The good experts, therefore, provide you with a guideline: equate a 500g fish to a surface area on the Grow bed, of $0.1m^2$.

6) Mind the Water Temperature

To be on the safe side, establish the fish species that adapt well to changing temperatures. If it becomes difficult to acquire those, then you better settle for those that require warm temperatures. This is because it is always easier and cheaper to warm up water than to cool it; using insulation, tank painting, and that kind of stuff.

7) Mind the Water pH

Work towards maintaining water pH of between 6.8 and 7.0 all through your system. This is the range that is ideal for both your fish and your plants.

And what happens, if unluckily, the pH falls below optimum range?

If you measure the pH, as you are wont to regularly, and you find it at 6.6 or below, boldly raise it using reasonable amounts of potassium carbonate or calcium hydroxide. In cases where you find it higher than the acceptable range, lower it using nitric acid; phosphoric acid; or any other acceptable hydroponic acid.

8) Think before you choose your fish species

This is what you need to base your thinking on:

- Do I want this fish for consumption or simply for display?
- How is the temperature of the water I am going to use?

- Am I interested in fish species of the herbivore family; carnivore family; or the omnivore family?

Keep in mind that fingerlings need their different area from mature fish; otherwise the mature ones might eat them up.

Conclusion

Thank you again for downloading this book!

I hope this book was able to help you to appreciate how easy it is to do farming using minimal resources of land and manure. It is also my hope that you would now consider rearing fish and growing vegetables using aquaponics, to boost the health of your family and make some money as well.

The next step is to assess the piece of space that you have and see the scale of aquaponic farming that you can do. It would also be a good idea to refer your family and friends to this book so that they, too, can benefit from the rich information provided on aquaponic farming.

Finally, if you enjoyed this book, please take the time to share your thoughts and post a review on Amazon. It'd be greatly appreciated!

Thank you and good luck!

Book # 2

Permaculture

The Ultimate Guide to Mastering Permaculture in 30 Minutes or Less

Copyright © 2015

All rights reserved. No part of this book may be reproduced in any form without permission in writing from the author. Reviewers may quote brief passages in reviews.

Disclaimer

No part of this publication may be reproduced or transmitted in any form or by any means, mechanical or electronic, including photocopying or recording, or by any information storage and retrieval system, or transmitted by email without permission in writing from the publisher.

While all attempts and efforts have been made to verify the information held within this publication, neither the author nor the publisher assumes any responsibility for errors, omissions, or opposing interpretations of the content herein.

This book is for entertainment purposes only. The views expressed are those of the author alone, and should not be taken as expert instruction or commands. The reader of this book is responsible for his or her own actions when it comes to reading the book.

Adherence to all applicable laws and regulations, including international, federal, state, and local governing professional licensing, business practices, advertising, and all other aspects of doing business in the US, Canada, or any other jurisdiction is the sole responsibility of the purchaser or reader.

Neither the author nor the publisher assumes any responsibility or liability whatsoever on the behalf of the purchaser or reader of these materials.

Any received slight of any individual or organization is purely unintentional.

Contents

Introduction

Chapter 1: Principles of Permaculture: Systems and Integral Approach

Chapter 2: Permaculture and Sustainable Environment

Chapter 3: Caring for People the Permaculture way

Chapter 4 Sustainable households wanted now

Chapter 5: Let us not fight Mother Earth, but embrace her

Chapter 6: How to solve our problems?

Conclusion

Introduction

First and foremost I want to thank you for downloading the book, *"PERMACULTURE: The Ultimate Guide to Mastering Permaculture in 30 Minutes or Less."*

In this book, you will learn what Permaculture is and how to apply the principles discussed herewith. The book will give you insights on caring for people, caring for the environment and sharing resources; the three maxims developed by Bill Mollison and David Holmgren, who are proponent of the Permaculture design concept. You will gain understanding on why it is important for everyone to apply these principles not tomorrow but TODAY, especially with the current environmental situation.

This book can guide you as a future Permaculturist in designing simple solutions to the ever-growing problem of un-sustainable environmental practices of people. The practices discussed in this book are so easy to follow and understand. You can even do these on your own backyard with low cost!

Ultimately, this book should serve as a revelation for everyone, that each person should be part of the solution for a sustainable planet. If you want the next generation to inherit a lovely and sustainable planet, then let us help you understand Permaculture and learn together through this book. Together let us apply the principles of the Permaculture movement now!

Thanks again for downloading this book, I hope you enjoy it!

Chapter 1: Principles of Permaculture: Systems and Integral Approach

Let us start our discussion of Permaculture with basic definitions. Permaculture is a design system, according to Bill Mollison as cited by Brown (2012) for creating sustainable human environments. Brown further discussed that the foundation of Permaculture design are rooted in different disciplines, which includes primarily Biology, Ecology, and Agriculture.

Practitioners of Permaculture combined the theories and foundations of these disciplines by with Engineering and Architecture design technologies, to produce a sustainable living environment or settlement for people (Brown, 2012.). Another definition of Permaculture asserts that this is the art and science of applying the principles and scientific theories of Biology with that of technological design, with the primary aim of making human settlement self-sustaining (McManus 2010).

To put it simply, we could describe Permaculture as learning how Mother Earth works and applying this observation and information through everyday human settlements to make living more self-sustaining and complementary with nature. Imagine yourself living in an environment where all activities and design of settlement mimics the way nature "designs" living spaces. That is Permaculture in a nutshell.

Permaculture is not a new idea, although the practice is still not that widespread as of today. It dates back in the 1970's when Australian pioneers Bill Mollison and David Holmgren developed the system as a response to the increasing number of environmental problems experienced during that period.

Some of these environmental problems in the 70's as discussed by DiTommaso are loss of wilderness and diversity, toxic waste, pollutions from power plants and factories. The extensive research and study made by Mollison and Holmgren in response to these environmental problems produced a radical way of thinking which they coined as "**Permaculture**."

Mollison and Holmgren came up with three key maxims to address those environmental issues that eventually defined the ethical foundation of Permaculture. Roth (2011) cites these in his article as follows:

1. Caring for the Earth;
2. Caring for People;

3. Fair share;

A person can grasps easily and understand what Permaculture is all about when thinking about these maxims. McManus emphasized that Permaculture design essentially adopts a sustainability perspective thereby suggesting that people who lives in the system and gets resources from the system must be prepared to give back what he has taken from nature.

This process of giving back what was taken should preserve the environment to be enjoyed by future generations (2010). The key here is to see everything as self-sustaining whole, where every element, even humans must abide by the laws of nature. This law of nature specifies that we should only take what we need and redistribute surplus. We should have a way to give back what we have taken so that the cycle will not be disrupted, thus maintaining sustainability of the whole system.

Linking Permaculture to Systems approach and Integral perspective, a prospective practitioner of the design must remember his role in the bigger scheme of things. Permaculture is not merely *permanent agriculture* where a person designs food production areas or living settlements aimed at maximizing production of basic human needs with less inputs and labor resources (Roth, 2011, Lowe, 2012).

A person must see himself as part of a bigger picture, a whole process, of which he is an integral or important member. Everything works in a Systems perspective in relation to and with each element. Permaculture becomes *permanent culture* where a person is not only on the receiving end of the bountiful resources available in the environment, but more importantly a steward of these resources to make sure that the future generations can survive.

Moore and Kearsley as cited by Puzziferro and Shelton (2008) describe Systems approach by liking it to a human body and its parts. In a Systems perspective, just like a human body, each part of the body plays an integral part in how the body works as a whole, some are more important than others, but it takes all parts to support a successful system (Puzziferro&Shelton, 2008).

For Permaculture design to be successful, a person should see himself as an important part of the whole process, not just a spectator from the outside looking in. He is not only designing permanent agriculture but he himself is also part of the design. A person must revolutionize the way he thinks about himself in relation to the environment. He must think of himself as both an object and subject of Permaculture design.

David Holmgren as cited by Roth (2011) in Permaculture 101 discussed the following principles that serve as cornerstones in the design of a sustainable environment. Holmgren considered these philosophies or *slogan* as checklist in the design of an ecological support system.

The following are the principles that form part of the Permaculture design approach:

1. Observe and interact.
2. Catch and store energy.
3. Obtain a yield.
4. Apply self-regulation and accept feedback.
5. Use and value renewable resources and services.
6. Produce no waste.

7. Design from patterns to details.

8. Integrate rather than segregate.

9. Use small and slow solutions.

10. Use and value diversity.

11. Use edges and value the marginal.

12. Creatively use and respond to change.

I will talk about these principles in detail and with specific examples as we go along the discussion of Permaculture in the succeeding chapters. For now, I encourage the reader to commit these ethical foundations and principles to heart to grasp fully the Permaculture design concept. I will go back to these principles and ethical foundation every now and then to drive a point across in the discourse. The succeeding chapters will give the reader a guide on how to start immediately with a Permaculture project with little resources at hand.

Chapter 2: Permaculture and Sustainable Environment

As discussed in the foregoing chapter, Permaculture borrows principles from Biology, particularly Ecology. Any science book would define Ecology as the branch of Biology that concerns with the interactions of organisms with one another and with the physical and chemical environment. It is very important to understand how each organism relates to one another and to know their places in the physical setting of the world.

This understanding is vital for the survival of each species. Remember in the preceding chapter, that McManus (2010) discussed the idea of Permaculture as adopting a *sustainability perspective*. This perspective is akin to Ecological thoughts as it suggests that human kind must know how to be able to give back what he has taken from the environment, in order for the next generation to benefit fully from the bountiful resources of nature.

Look at the food chain for example. From simple one-cell organisms to more complex higher forms, each has a part to do to perpetuate the food cycle and eventually the cycle of life. Let us take this simple example of interaction between three organisms: blades of grass, a cow and a human.

A cow for example eats grass, and then the human butchered the same cow for meat for human consumption. If the human eats more cows than being produced or breed, then there might be resources depletion, and worst may cause extinction of the cow. Cows are not only producers of meat, but also of milk and other milk by-products such as cheese. If cows no longer graze on Earth, these cow by-products will also cease to exist (ouch!) causing imbalance in the ecological system.

If cows do not exist anymore, who then will eat the grass and weeds? What if weeds grow at an alarming rate and would not be contained? The rapid growth of weeds would affect other plant species. Other plants may die because of the weeds. I know the food chain is more complex than the given example and ecological imbalance is cause by many factors, but for the purpose of simple illustration, I hope this example may suffice to drive a point across. Taking out one element in the system can cause problems in the other components, though these problems may not manifest early on because of other alternatives available.

You can also compare this to the "Butterfly effect" as discussed in Chaos Theory where according to the said theory a flutter of the wings of a butterfly from one part of the world can cause tremendous catastrophe at the other side of the planet. Butterfly effect is a phenomenon according to dictionary.com where "a small perturbation in the initial condition of a system can result in large changes in later conditions."

With the wide spread consumerism and higher materialism of the world, people is being insulated with the current reality that resources in the environment are slowly being depleted.

Mollison and Holmgren's principles of Permaculture state, hat peoples' needs should be within the ecological limits set by nature. In other words, only get what you need in order to survive and have a good quality of life, of course not at the expense of other components in the ecological system. (Essence of Permaculture, accessed from permacultureprinciples.com on April 13, 2015). These Permaculture principles may seem like common sense tenets; unfortunately, people ignore or deliberately forget these all in the name of materialism and consumerism. We have to remember that as humans, we are also govern by the same scientific laws that govern the material universe and even evolution of life itself (Essense..., 2013).

Simply put, even if human are on top of the food chain and may somehow feel *important* in the cycle of life, the same rule of the universe still applies. Natural resources supply a person's necessities. Though there are synthetic resources available, still majority of these sources has its foundation in nature. If nature fails to provide for these necessities, then possibly, humans may also cease to exist. That may be an extreme circumstance, but nonetheless highly probable if we continue with our unsustainable ways and lifestyle.

Permaculture design aims to make available a sustainable environment where needs of inhabitants are well provided for. When a person wants to design a human settlement with Permaculture as the main strategy or approach, that person must be aware of all the resources the settlement will need to have a viable, sustainable, healthy and vibrant community. The designer would also need to know where to get these resources and how the community or household can be self-reliant or self-sustaining without adverse ecological implications. These Permaculture communities are design to provide for themselves their needs base on the careful planning of consumption and generation of inputs.

The next chapter will detail the role of humans in Permaculture design and development. There will be discussions on ensuing chapters on humans' relationship with other elements of the system to see how this relation affects the action of each component to achieve synergy in nature. Humans play a particularly important role since most of the environmental problems that Permaculture design tries to address are brought about by the unsustainable practices of humans in the environment.

Chapter 3: Caring for People the Permaculture way

Attitude is important in practicing Permaculture according to Jeff Brown (2012). In designing sustainable environment that mimics how nature works, a person must not only think of himself, but also of other people and other elements that are part of the Eco-system. As discussed in the previous chapters of this book, people or humans are very important or integral part of the Permaculture design. A person is not only the doer or designer, but also the subject of the design itself. Each person is part of the system and the system will be very successful if all parts are working as one. Brown (2012) further reinforced the idea that Permaculture combines our physical, mental, emotional, and spiritual selves into the process of designing our lifestyles.

He asserts that if people omit any one of the element stated above from the equation, we are not allowing ourselves to be fully human. Following the Permaculture tenets, those who would like to practice and do Permaculture designing must see to it that living settlements combine these features as discussed by Brown. The way a person lives his life must show his awareness of his role in the whole eco-system. He must know where he stands and what others expected of him in relation to the eco-system. Even the slightest alteration in lifestyle can have an adverse impact in the environment as what is currently experience worldwide with the dawn of industrialization and massive transport systems.

By knowing how different components act and react with each other and how the combination of these elements works, we will ensure that there will be symbiosis among these parts. This will not only make living more sustainable for current generation but would also contribute for the overall well-being of future generations.

If a person put into heart and practices these Permaculture principles, he will always see himself as part of a whole system, where life is a web. Given this perspective, we can see that Permaculture also borrows principles from Sociology and other Social Sciences when we situate a person relative to the society or community. If a person knows his place and role in the society and in the larger eco-system, he would not be consumed by the need to accumulate and utilize beyond his needs because he knows that another person or another organism also requires the resources being made available to him by Mother Earth.

He is also aware that whatever resources he takes from nature, he should be able to give it back somehow. He will be *practicing self-regulation and feedback* (McManus, 2010). In other words, Permaculture will make a person see himself in relation to other people and other organism in the grand scheme of things. By knowing how he affects other elements of the system, a person can regulate himself and apply the feedback he receives. Self-awareness is therefore of great importance to the teaching and practice of Permaculture (McManus, 2010).

Talking about self-awareness and caring for other people, I remember a story regarding a native resident (a local) of a community and a visitor or outsider. A professor told this story during one of our community development classes in college.

The story goes like this. Once there was a native resident tasked to join a visitor as he goes around during a community visit. The visitor made the trip to assess the resources available in the local resident's community. As the visit progresses around the community, the local resident stops by a tree bearing fruits and picked one ripe fruit from a low lying branch. The local resident munches on the fruit and eventually gets going. The visitor stopped the local resident and asked why he got only one fruit where in fact the tree has plenty of ripe fruits. "It looks like no one owns the tree anyway so why not get more of the fruits" said the visitor.

The local resident looks at the visitor with puzzlement evident in his face. He said, "Why would I get more when I need only one to satisfy my need, in this case my hunger." The visitor counter that the local resident can get the fruits and sell it to merchants so he can have more money to buy more things such as food, clothing or a new house. The local resident replied, "how about the next person who will pass this way? What if that person is also hungry as I was? If I harvest all the fruits, he will be left with nothing to satisfy his hunger. He might get ill or worst he might die. What satisfaction would that give if I knew that I was the cause of death of my brother?" The visitor was dumbstruck with the logic of the local resident and felt ashamed for even suggesting such practice. The story ends there.

The moral of the story as discussed by our professor is that for communities to thrive and be sustainable, each person must care for one another. No one should monopolize resources for own satisfaction and enjoyment. Before even thinking of ways to introduce new technology or new way of living, a person must be aware of what is currently available in his environment vis-à-vis his needs to survive and to have a good quality of life.

Of course, his needs should not trample or impinge on the needs of other people or even other Biological species. Everyone should enjoy the resources available in nature based on his needs and the needs of other organisms in the system. Everyone's needs are important and everyone's necessities should be taken care of and not neglected.

In Permaculture designed settlements, sustainability must come from within (Roth, 2011). Since a person will be designing the sustainable household, he should first look from within himself before venturing out, as it is possible for a person to have initially a lot of perspective or ideas contrary to the ethical foundations and principles of Permaculture.

To have a successful Permaculture designed community, a potential practitioner should ask, *Am I prepared to change the way I think of people and things and to change eventually how I see myself in relation to others? Am I prepared to embraced the principle of caring for people, caring for earth and redistribute surplus to one's own need?*

If the answer is positive to these questions, then a person can practice Permaculture with high degree of success. If at any time a person has doubts or cannot answer the said question with high conviction, then do not fret. Changing of perspective does not happen overnight. Small steps in the direction of accepting Permaculture principles can spell a big difference. The key in embracing Permaculture is to *think solutions, not barriers* to execution (Roth, 2011).

Chapter 4 Sustainable households wanted now

After discussing the foundations, ethics and principles behind Permaculture, and after thorough introspection, the potential practitioner should answer this question next: *are we ready to embrace these Permaculture tenets and maxims?* With the growing environmental issues and unsustainable practices that are utilize all over the world, I think everyone should answer an unequivocal YES! Yes, we should be ready to embrace Permaculture as a way of life.

So now, you may want to ask, how should you start making your living settlement more sustainable the Permaculture way? I would suggest the first step should be reviewing and committing by heart the ethical principles of Permaculture as describe in the previous chapters of this book.

Remember this: *care for others, care for Earth and redistribute surplus* (Holmgren as cited by McManus, 2010). It may be useful to make a checklist that deals with the practical application of the principles of Permaculture. Let us take the first principle for example, which is *Observe and Interact*.

What does this principle tells a Permaculture designer? Primarily, the designer should be aware of nature's way of doing things such as food production, waste management, even the types of biodiversity available in a certain area given a certain weather condition. A designer must learn and interact with nature as McManus described to so that design solutions are applicable with the situation at hand. In short, in designing sustainable household, the way nature operates is the best blueprint for any Permaculture designer. Roth reminds us that in Ecology everyone has a place in the system and exists in relation to everyone else (2011).

These relationships give individual elements in nature meaning and value, said Roth. To concretize this principle, a designer should see the location of every aspect of his living design in conjunction with other components and see how these different elements complement each other. Take for example the relative location of an organic food garden from the main house and the existence of a poultry farm. By combining these elements, the potential Permaculture practitioner can design his settlement by observing the needs of these different components. He can react then base on what he observed. From our example, we can probably locate the main house a little further from the poultry farm to avoid the smell of organic waste excreted, but the food garden may come between the house and the poultry farm so that these organic wastes becomes fertilizer for the garden. Roth also observe that if gardens are near the house, there is a higher chance for people increasing their number of hours tending to it, which is beneficial for the proper caring of the plants. One must consider the relative location of each component in the Permaculture design to maximize each element's potential to contribute to the whole eco-system.

In designing sustainable household, a person can also look at the different sources for his needs and combine these to create a *redundancy in design* (Roth, 2011). By designing different sources for a persons' living requirements, the person will not only reduce dependency on any one kind of supply but would also help the environment to continuously provide in a sustainable manner, all of the needs of the inhabitants of the household. One example at present is the big dependency from power plants to supply household with needed electricity.

Consider this scenario: what if the power plant that supplies electricity broke down? What would happen to the household that depends on it? To avoid this scenario from happening, Permaculture design will make sure that there are multiple sources for the needs of the household, such as food, energy, water, etc. Slowly there are households now that combine different sources for these needs. Take for example the source of light for each household. With the advent of solar power, house designer are now incorporating solar harvesting tools to their homes to try to collect solar energy to power a household. This will reduce dependency on one source of electricity and other energy requirements of the household. This design follows the principle of Permaculture where a designer should develop a system or strategy that allows resources to be collected when they are in abundance so they can be redistributed and utilize when they are needed the most (McManus, 2010).

Sometimes, as a person we deal too much with hindrances rather than thinking of creative solutions to a problem. As discussed by Brown (2012), with Permaculture, a person is encouraged to think of ways to address and overcome common barriers to a sustainable system by observing the following:

1. Observe relative location and placement;
2. Important functions supported by different elements;
3. Diversity and polyculture is encourage;
4. There should be appropriate use of technology;
5. Sustainable food production;

To be fully sustainable, a household must also encourage greater participation from the bigger community. Most of the ecological problems faces today, as discussed in previous chapters are the result of people or households that do not see themselves and their actions in relation to others. It will be very hard for individuals and their own household to design a fully sustainable system if the community outside their household still practices unsustainable acts.

Let us look in to the management of solid waste in the community as an example. A household may practice segregation and even composting at home because members of that household know the importance of that practice in maintaining sustainability. However, the greater majority of families outside in the community do not care how they throw their wastes.

In the end, if the unsustainable practice of the neighbors persists, then there is a big possibility that even those who practice proper waste management may become victims of improper waste disposal. Therefore, potential Permaculture designer must also take time to approach community leaders or authorities to discuss his plans for his immediate community and probably ask for their support to ensure environmental sustainability.

Chapter 5: Let us not fight Mother Earth, but embrace her

At this point, we have established that Permaculture draws its ethics and principles from the different disciplines, such as Biology, Social Sciences and Agriculture. The learning theories from these disciplines combined with Engineering and Architecture should create a design system that is both ecologically sound and sustainable according to Permaculture standards. Going back to how nature works is one of the objectives of Permaculture design household or settlement.

In achieving this sustainability, again Permaculture designer should keep in mind the following maxim: care for people, care for Earth and re-distribute surplus to one's need. People should not forget these, instead keep these truths close to heart.

At the core of Permaculture, there is the strong clamor to go back and embrace nature. As a person is engaged in Permaculture design, he should first learn from the way the Earth sustains herself. Since the beginning of time, there is an assumption that everything that we ever need; we can get from the environment, which is why we call our planet **Mother Earth.**

The Earth is nurturing, even the Genesis story confirms this. The story goes like this. When the first man and woman were created, they were given a garden where they can get everything that they would ever need. Unfortunately, man in his lofty ways and greediness, yearns to have more. The story sadly ends with the first people banished from the lush garden and succumbing to toiling the Earth just to survive. The first people had everything, but they throw it all away all in the name of wanting more and being more.

The rapid globalization, higher capitalism, industrialization, and the drive of people to consume more than what they really need; this is slowly driving our planet to this sorry state of decay and unsustainable future.

We are currently experiencing the fact that we need to toil hard just to get our basic needs and survive. Our food, our water, oxygen, the roof above our heads; they were produced with man's technology but this technology is unsustainable. It goes against nature's way of production and cycle of life. The dawn of the Industrial Revolution saw the rapid changes in the way people interact with nature and the resources available. Holmgren, in Essence of Permaculture (permacultureprinciples.com) assume that the survival of our species will greatly depend on how we manage our consumption and generation of resources (2011).

To embrace nature and live with its abundance, I got the following statements from Barrette's article (2011), which is very helpful for Permaculturist who wishes to ally with nature and not against her. Elizabeth Barrette (2011) discussed these fundamental ideas to help potential practitioners of Permaculture to get started:

1. Start where you are and use what you already have;
2. Remember that everything is connected;
3. Trees sweat so humans do not have to;
4. Natures produces bounty;
5. Get out of the way;

A person who wishes to start a Permaculture design project does not need a big budget to proceed as stated by Barrette. As discussed in the article, a designer should check what is readily available in his immediate surroundings. If there are free seeds available through a community seedling bank, then start there. Often times Permaculture project does not get off the ground because the designer focuses more on the impediments rather than the creative solutions available. It will help if you make an inventory of the resources you have already at your disposal.

Start working from there. You do not also need to start big and transform all your land and household into a Permaculture designed settlement. Start with a small organic garden, or flower patch. Just remember what Barrette discussed, that everything is connected. So before you introduce a technology or architectural design to your project, ask yourself this question: *what would this structure achieved in the overall Permaculture system? Will adding this element help in the symbiotic relationship of all components or will it disrupt the natural cycle?*

Upon pondering the answers to these questions, a designer should see and take stock of the functions of each element in the system. It would be beneficial if a certain resource, such as a tree, herb or shrub can do multiple-functions, such as providing shade, fruits, insect repellant, etc. Try to research as much as you can on the caring and tending of flora and fauna before incorporating the species into your Permaculture project. This way, you can maximize the resources you currently have. You would want the different parts of your project to complement and not compete with each other for attention and resources.

Remember also that nature has its ways of producing enough for everyone. As Barrette emphasized, nature can produce bountiful resources enough for everybody's needs. Take note what your household members requires and learn how your household's ecosystem works together. By grouping complementary parts collectively, the design can maximize the symbiotic relationship that can benefit both humans and nature according to Barrette (2011).

If in doubt on how to proceed, it is best *to get out of the way* or let nature takes its course as said by Barrette. This means a designer should let nature runs its course. Learn how nature takes care of the different elements in the system. Most of the environmental problems we have at present stems from the fact that human trample upon this system organized by nature. For example, because we want more food, bigger portions and rapidly growing trees to keep up with our needs, we would spray the land with chemicals to aid in production. Unfortunately, this practice causes problems with the land itself. These chemicals are not naturally part of the system and its introduction produces an imbalance in the ecology and sustainability of the land.

It is time to stop being a *rebel child* of Mother Earth; instead, every person should start becoming a loving and caring scion of this planet. It is the only way to ensure that our specie would eventually survive and future generations can inherit a lush, livable and nurturing environment.

Chapter 6: How to solve our problems?

Einstein: "We cannot solve our problems with the same level of thinking that created them"

I really like the quote above and I think it is very much applicable in our discussion of Permaculture. Consider this, if Einstein thinks the way people think during his time, he might not have discovered the formula for relativity. Remember $E=mc^2$? This formula paved the way for the discovery of other forms or sources of energy, which help fuel the development of civilizations.

Unfortunately, some scientists abused this knowledge and came up with destructive use of the same formula. Regardless, what I am driving at in conjunction with Permaculture design concept is that people need to think *outside of the box* if he wants to be successful in its implementation. Permaculture engages the practitioner in thinking of solutions rather than barriers or hindrances.

It makes you reflect on where you stand in the grand scheme of things and think if your role in maintaining ecological balance. If our thoughts run just as our ancestors did, the same ancestors who advocated rapid industrialization and higher consumerism in the name of development, then we cannot properly addressed all the environmental problems we face today. Particularly, we cannot think of ecological sustainability by thinking of the same solutions as before. If you conduct your life every day with the same level of thinking, then Einstein's quote is very much applicable.

We want to reduce our carbon footprint, we want to eliminate pollution and we want to manage how we generate waste. However, are we ready to change the way we live our lives? Beck Lowe (2012) said, it is very important to set an example of an alternative, more sustainable lifestyle, but you should be prepared to do it with conviction as it often involves going against entrenched gender stereotypes and even government regulations.

In her efforts to design her own settlement the Permaculture way, Lowe often had to do things herself, change the way she uses electricity, modify her food production and consumption, among other activities. Generally, to achieve a successful Permaculture designed environment where she knows her lifestyle complements natural order and nature's supplies her needs, Lowe needs to sacrifice and change the way she thinks and does things.

There are so many protest movements and activist clamoring for the government to address the growing problem of pollution, urban decay, climate change and other environmental problems, but deep inside, some of these same people are not willing to let go of old practices that are not sustainable.

In the end, people become frustrated because they see no solution from the government officials to the rapidly deteriorating environment, and yet they cannot forego the simple act of using a plastic drinking straw or using a plastic bag during shopping to prevent the accumulation unmanaged solid waste. This is quite ironic and counter intuitive. Now, there is a call to think radically, beyond what has been practiced in the past to ensure successful implementation of Permaculture designed household. Lowe further asserts that her experience with Permaculture design course is both life changing and empowering (2012).

The course help her identify the elements that would support her goal of having a low-carbon, sustainable lifestyle, human-scale society. The question is, are we ready to embrace this simple, sustainable lifestyle?

Before starting on the project, I suggest a moment of reflection for the main proponent. The designer needs to take stack of all his prior knowledge and understanding of Biology, particularly Ecology, biodiversity, systems and integral approach, even human relations, technology and eco-systems design. He should compare the information and learning gathered with the principles and ethical standards of Permaculture as discussed by Bill Mollison and David Holmgren. If there are concepts that are not align or not congruent with the sustainable approach advocated by Permaculture design, the proponent then should be willing to take a leap and try to see the other perspective.

In other words, the designer must be willing addressed and see the problem under a new light, in this case under the "Permaculture light." With this approach, there is a higher chance that the proponent would successfully implement and sustain a Permaculture designed human settlement according to ethical standards and principles developed by Mollison and Holmgren. As the proponent goes about the design of his living space, it is also important to consider doing it or going about it in small, but deliberate portions, rather than tackling large projects all at once. A person might get overwhelmed with the magnitude of the project, especially since we are introducing some radical ideas about working with nature for household sustainability.

If you are still new with the concept and just trying it out, it would be better to start small and work your way towards bigger areas. Of course, keep in mind the bigger picture. We want a self-sustaining and ecologically sound household, so even if we start small, and with few components in the design, still these elements must be seen in the light of the bigger Permaculture project. Eventually the main objective is for a person to be able to design his living quarters where he can closely mimic nature's way of producing his needs and ensuring sustainability not only for present occupants but for future generations to come.

Give Permaculture a chance to make you see that this can be achieved. We can have a sustainable future if we can change the way we see and do things in relation to other elements in nature. Let Permaculture open our eyes to the possibility that human settlements can thrive under low inputs, producing less carbon-foot print and still able to provide the needs of humans to have a good quality of life. It is just a matter of changing perspective.

Conclusion

Thank you again for downloading this book!

I hope this book was able to help you to understand the principles behind Permaculture. You can now apply these principles in your everyday lives to make your household more environment-friendly and sustainable. Remember that Permaculture is not just "Permanent Agriculture," but "Permanent Culture" or a way of life.

The next step upon successful completion of this book is to research for more information and thorough discussions of these Permaculture maxims and principles. You may consult *Introduction to Permaculture* by Bill Mollison and *Permaculture: Principles and Pathways Beyond Sustainability* by David Holmgren. After gathering information, you may want to apply what you have learned and start your own Permaculture design household or settlement.

Finally, if you enjoyed this book, please take the time to share your thoughts and post a review on Amazon. It would be greatly appreciated!

Thank you and good luck!

Made in the USA
San Bernardino, CA
29 March 2018